DENTAL DISRUPTION

THE DECADE THAT CHANGED DENTISTRY

Learn How You Can Achieve the
Practice of Your Dreams
by Embracing Change and
Implementing the
New Dental Marketing Paradigm

JACKIE ULASEWICH

COPYRIGHT

OUR "WHY"

We believe in thinking differently from mass marketing groups and standing up against corporate dentistry. We do this by helping independent practices to build genuine relationships with patients, create and manage positive reputations by utilizing online resources, and retain their current patients (who are their greatest untapped assets). We achieve all of this by creating custom, relatable, personalized, and distinctly different campaigns that reflect the needs and personalities of each individual practice.

"Marketing is no longer about the stuff that you make, but about the stories you tell."

- Seth Godin

FOREWORD

The last decade began with little to no marketing of dental practices and ended with an explosion of digital marketing opportunities. These new opportunities can be incorporated into strategies that are applicable regardless of the size of your practice or how long established. Opportunities are abundant whether you:

- are opening your first practice,

- have an established practice and need to build business in order to bring in an associate and eventually retire, or

- you want to develop marketing know–how to make needed changes.

Creating the correct digital presence can help your practice to succeed as much or more than either the corporate dental operations or your neighboring dentist.

But the online landscape is oversaturated and competition is fierce. Choosing your marketing agency may be one of the most important decisions you will ever make because there are many marketing agencies that deliver unoriginal, templated materials that will not help your practice stand out above your competition.

In *Dental Disruption* you will see how far dental marketing has progressed in the last decade. You will learn how some savvy doctors are incorporating new digital marketing strategies to attract the type of patients they want and build their ideal practice faster. You will find solid ideas and tips for how you can begin to benefit from the "dental disruption." And, perhaps most importantly, you will acquire a checklist that will arm you with the qualifications you should look for when choosing a marketing agency.

ABOUT JACKIE ULASEWICH

When I was seeking jobs in marketing and business development after completing college, I was contacted by a dental laboratory to be interviewed. To prepare for the interview, I visited a local dental practice that happened to have a lab box from that very laboratory. They graciously allowed me to keep it. I used that lab box to prepare what I was fairly sure would be a one-of-a-kind "reminder" of the marketing skills I would bring to their position. In one of the lab box impression trays I wrote my first name, on the second tray I wrote my last, and on the lab script I wrote, "I wanted to leave a lasting impression." I also prepared myself with all the information I could about their business and their goals.

I was interviewed by a panel of five people. At the end of the interview I slid the lab box with my customized message across the table. This calculated risk helped me to land my first job in the dental industry.

Once I was hired, I became a student again. I spent ten years observing and doing market research in hundreds of practices across the United States and quickly became an expert in my field. With my newfound knowledge, I was able to assess the needs and struggles of individual practices as well as identify the fallibilities of the marketing industry itself.

I watched the marketing industry become more corporate and more concerned with their own needs rather than those of their clients. The time was right for a dental marketing business that was passionate about helping, considerate of the solo practitioner, and dedicated to implementing marketing strategies that work. I wanted to capitalize on the needs and personality of each of my clients and provide them with something personable, well-planned, and customized to make them stand out among the rest. To realize this dream I had to move away from corporate marketing to start my own small business.

When I started my own marketing firm, My Dental Agency, I suddenly found myself in charge of billing, bookkeeping, accounting—all things I did not have the know-how or time for. I opted to hire an accountant to handle my books.

Your situation is likely similar. You went to school to become a dentist, but dental school did not prepare you for the business side of establishing and maintaining a dental practice, much less the now essential marketing aspects to building that practice.

While it may be tempting to hire a large marketing company, if they don't customize their approach, integrate all your digital campaigns, and help you to enhance your relationships outside your practice, then you are simply wasting your money and you are not serving the needs of your patients.

After years of experience I have created philosophies and practices that work for both my business and those of my clients:

- Every marketing strategy is carefully crafted for each client based on a comprehensive, customized approach to their unique business needs.

- We bring in new business, but we focus on enhancing relationships with existing patients.

- We integrate marketing solutions and use multiple channels that work together seamlessly. Facebook, blog posts, websites, remarketing, paid ads and emails work together to create a complete strategy.

- We create fun, relatable, and unique marketing tools that stand out in a sea of repetitive, templated, and uninspiring materials.

As a dental practice marketing expert, I know the importance of creating an overall marketing strategy that focuses on the unique needs of your practice. You need a strategy that integrates the different delivery channels to deliver a seamless, consistent message to prospective patients. You need a program that will deliver the ideal patients your practice needs to thrive. This is my specialty.

LET'S GET DIGITAL!

DENTALDISRUPTION.COM/CALL

If you've been resisting the transition from traditional marketing to digital, hesitate no more. My Dental Agency has helped countless dentists just like you make the leap. What's more, we're in it for the long haul. From your initial FREE breakthrough session to achieving the vision you've always had for your practice, we'll be there with you. You'll have more time to do what you're great at, and we'll take care of the rest.

Contact us today at DentalDisruption.com/call

Table of Contents

About Jackie Ulasewich .... *xiii*

Introduction .... *xix*

Chapter One...*1*
Learning to Adapt in a World of Change

Chapter Two...*7*
The Birth of the Digital Age

Chapter Three *13*
Digital Marketing 2.0 — A New Approach

Chapter Four...*41*
TheMarketing Disruptions That Are a Detriment to Your Practice

Chapter Five *53*
Client Success Stories

Chapter Six...*75*
Marketing Campaign Success Stories

Chapter Seven...*99*
A Final Word

INTRODUCTION

It's 2006.

Dr. Jones has had his dental practice, located in a nicer part of his town, for eight-and-a-half years. He is thinking about the future and wants to grow his business. He has some technology that other local dentists don't and he wants to leverage that advantage to round up some new patients. But he knows very little about marketing and he hesitates to do anything that might be perceived as too grand.

He realizes that he needs help so he places a call to the editor of a small neighborhood newsletter and inquires about advertising in her publication. He and the editor agree that the use of color will help draw potential patients to view the ad. They craft a general message incorporating his practice name and number in bold print and end the call. Dr. Jones sits back and eagerly awaits the new patients this ad will bring.

The ad comes out the following Monday. The phone doesn't ring, but Dr. Jones is realistic and knows that the results won't be immediate. He waits a week before he hears from a lead that learned of his practice through the ad. Before the next issue is published, Dr. Jones hears from a total of three new patients as a direct result of his marketing efforts. This is a start, but if he's going to relocate to a larger building, he's going to need far more patients to fill those extra treatment suites.

In 2006, this type of marketing was effective—to a certain extent.

Dr. Jones was able to recognize the need for more patients, but the scope of his imagination was limited to what he knew.

Radio spots, television commercials, and billboards were common, but too expensive and too showy in an industry that frowned on overt advertising. Posting an ad in the local newspaper or sending out postcards were also options, but at the time, almost all concentrated marketing efforts were taboo.

Dr. Jones selected the neighborhood newsletter option because it was recommended by an out–of–state colleague who had a positive experience with this type of advertising and it was the least likely to be judged by his colleagues as undignified. Using a method like this allowed him to reach a limited audience without having to splash his name on every bus stop bench, billboard, and in local TV commercials. It was a low–risk attempt that, at the time, helped him subtly get his name out into the community.

✶✶✶✶✶✶✶✶✶✶✶✶✶✶✶✶

It's now 2017.

Dr. Jones is looking at his appointment book. It's not as full as he'd like it to be. He knows that if he wants to sell his practice and retire in the next 15 years, something will need to change.

In order to attract the right associate dentist who might want to buy, his practice needs to be thriving. He needs additional patients–patients who are willing to prioritize their dental health and invest in treatment.

Desperate to build his practice, he sends an email to the newsletter editor and asks for an even bigger ad. Marketing in this way is not the most effective, but it's what he knows. Sticking with what we know is the more comfortable option—but sometimes that is akin to doing nothing at all.

Dr. Jones Has an "Aha" Moment

When Dr. Jones gets home he sorts the daily mail into two piles: bills and trash. He takes the bills into his home office and throws everything else in the trash. Later he thinks about everything he put into the trash. When was the last time he actually looked at mail that wasn't a bill or a holiday card? When does anybody take time to look through the "junk mail" that is delivered by the United States Postal Service almost every day?

It hits him like a ton of bricks. No one is seeing his ads!

He recognizes that the world has become far more fast-paced, and time has become a commodity. In fact, every time he looks around his reception room, his patients are looking down at their phones. Patients have even interrupted treatment simply because they heard a notification alert on their phones. He's been at dinners with colleagues, dinner with family, and even dined alone, and in every situation, phones were on top of the tables next to the water glasses and bread baskets.

Time for a Change

It is true that browsing through physical mail has been replaced with ultra-fast browsing on the Internet, and it's time for Dr. Jones to leave his comfort zone and adapt. If he doesn't adapt he may fail to attract new patients and quality cases in enough numbers to maintain, much less grow, his practice as he has dreamed.

But what are the new ways to market his practice in the digital age? What are the best choices for his practice? How can he decide on a marketing plan that will be successful? Can he do it alone, or should he hire a marketing expert? And, ultimately, will Dr. Jones be able to jump out of his comfort zone, let loose of old methods and embrace the new? Read on to learn the answer to these questions and more.

DID YOU KNOW?

More than **46% of Americans** will check their smartphone before getting out of bed.

(TECH TIMES, 2017) • SOURCE: HTTPS://WWW.HUBSPOT.COM/MARKETING-STATISTICS

CHAPTER ONE

Learning to Adapt in a World of Change

CHAPTER ONE

Learning to Adapt in a World of Change

In the past decade, there have been transitions and disruptions in the world of dental marketing that are affecting your practice. The global community has become increasingly dependent on technology and any business that wants to continue to thrive must adapt. That's not to say that traditional marketing methods have become completely obsolete. But they have morphed into something new and more accessible to the people you're trying to reach.

If you take your marketing seriously and understand how vital it is to have an online presence, this book is exactly what you need to open your eyes to the world of possibilities available to market your practice in this competitive environment. You will learn which changes have occurred and why it's important to adapt to and even embrace the new digital marketing era.

"Back in My Day"
A Little History

When I began working with dentists in 2005, online marketing had not yet penetrated the industry; even higher education was having trouble figuring out how to incorporate technology. In fact, when I was a student, my professors were still using chalkboards. When I returned years later to give a presentation, every classroom had its own smartboard.

Now, students are required to take courses on social media and other forms of technology and they have an understanding of cookies, caching, and cloud computing. Because tech hadn't completely caught on at my university and conventional marketing was still in use, everything I learned when I earned my BA in Marketing focused on traditional methods. Most of the practices I worked with were using snail mail to communicate with patients, and appointments were handwritten into appointment books. Websites, if they had one, were rudimentary and they were sending coupons via MailPak, buying ad space on bus benches—and that is just for starters. Many dentists, particularly those with well–established reputations, weren't advertising at all because word–of–mouth alone was growing their practice.

The changes that occurred in the marketing industry forced me to learn how to adapt. After all, digital marketing is still marketing, just with new tools. So, I attended trainings and spent countless hours immersed in all the information I could find. From utilizing social media to finding a reliable and user-friendly automated email service and keeping up with all of the new updates to websites, I absorbed all of the changes that the digital world had to offer.

As a fellow business owner, I can safely say that my willingness to change not only helped me stay relevant in an ever–changing industry, but helped me grow my marketing business, as well. In fact, in this ever–changing world of technology, my team and I hold monthly trainings for each other, known as GOEO (Get

Our Education On), in order to keep up with trends and new technologies.

The good news is that when you are ready to take the next giant step forward in marketing your practice but need a mentor to help, my team and I have the expertise you can depend on to create the custom campaign ideal for your practice. And now may be just the time for you to take that leap and seek the help you need. After all, your patients hire an expert to take care of their teeth, and an expert is "just what the doctor ordered" to solve your marketing needs, too.

LET'S GET DIGITAL!

DENTALDISRUPTION.COM/CALL

If you've been resisting the transition from traditional marketing to digital, hesitate no more. My Dental Agency has helped countless dentists just like you make the leap. What's more, we're in it for the long haul. From your initial FREE breakthrough session to achieving the vision you've always had for your practice, we'll be there with you. You'll have more time to do what you're great at, and we'll take care of the rest.

Contact us today at DentalDisruption.com/call

CHAPTER TWO

The Birth of the Digital Age

CHAPTER TWO

The Birth of the Digital Age

Beginning in 2005, my marketing position with the dental lab put me in touch with hundreds, if not thousands, of dental practices across the country. Through the relationships I built with the doctors who owned these businesses, I was able to see the inner workings of what it took to run a practice—including how they marketed themselves (if at all). From Texas to New Hampshire and Minnesota to North Carolina my observations were the same; regardless of the state, region, or demographic, these dentists had one thing in common—lack of digital resources. At that point, marketing was considered to be taboo for most practices, particularly practices that offered specialized cosmetic and restorative treatments.

At that time:

- Word-of-mouth was the ultimate way to attract new patients, and because word-of-mouth leaves no digital trail, online reputation management was of little concern.

- As I am sure you remember, most practices were closed on Fridays and sometimes closed for an additional half day or full day during the week. The assumption was that the quality patients they desired would make time to visit their practice.

- Many dentists preferred to play it safe by foregoing websites, opting instead to disseminate their information via pamphlets and advertisements in local newspapers and neighborhood newsletters.

- The marketing that was utilized tended to be very straightforward: "Cleaning and X-Rays for $79. Call our office today." This very direct approach failed to incorporate creativity and the personality of the practice.

In the beginning of the century, the Internet was still in its infancy. Homes that had computers still used dial-up connections. E-commerce was a new and exciting way to buy things, but was only offered by a few companies. And while it had been in existence for over six years, Amazon.com wasn't our go-to for everything from birthday gifts to groceries.

The Rise of Digital Advertising

Now, not only do we have computers in our homes and offices, we carry them in our pockets. Smartphones, tablets, and even watches provide us with instant access to information. Instead of having a face–to–face conversation with a friend about which lawnmower is best or which carpet cleaning company offers the best deals, we do a quick search on the Consumer Reports site or reach out to our "friends" on Facebook for an immediate referral. The very way we communicate has changed forever. Don't believe me? Try going without your phone for two days.

Aside from our ever increasing reliance on technology, corporate dentistry has infiltrated the market. As a result, concepts such as patient trust, quality of care, highly skilled doctors and team members, and word-of-mouth were replaced or retooled in favor of flashy websites devoid of personalized content to lure in patients.

Private Practices Must Adapt to Compete with Corporate Dental Clinics

While corporate dentistry cannot truly be compared to private practice, it still plays a role in how you market. Because these dentists are backed by major health corporations with deep pockets, they can saturate the market with their ads—flashy TV commercials, billboards on every corner, and radio commercials that strive to get potential patients interested in the corporate practice.

Unfortunately, John Q. Public doesn't know the difference between private practice and corporate dentistry—all they see is the advertising. It's up to you to use marketing to educate consumers and let them know why your practice is the right choice. Using technology to market a private practice levels the playing field a bit—even if you and the corporate practice down the street are barely playing the same sport.

DID YOU KNOW?

Harvard Business School Assistant Professor Michael Luca designed a study to see if online reviews affected a business's bottom line. He quantified the significance of Yelp reviews and concluded that each ratings star added on a review translated to anywhere from a 5 to 9% effect on revenues (depending on the control variables and means of estimation).

HTTP://WWW.RESTAURANTBUSINESSONLINE.COM/MARKETING/IGNORE-SOCIAL-MEDIA-ONLINE-REVIEWS-YOUR-OWN-RISK

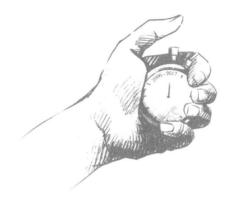

CHAPTER THREE

Digital Marketing 2.0 — A New Approach

CHAPTER THREE

Digital Marketing 2.0 — A New Approach

We can combine the best practices and ideals from the past decade. We can simultaneously emphasize the traditional ideals of dentistry and use technology, not only to bring new patients aboard, but to retain existing patients, as well. The methods may be different, but the end results are the same.

This chapter highlights the major changes that have occurred in dental marketing and illustrates what digital marketing can do for your practice.

PATIENT TRUST

THEN

Until recently, a patient knew they could trust you when they learned about you through others in the community. That was enough to get them to call for an appointment. The stylishly framed degree on your wall gave them the confidence they needed to trust that you knew your stuff. When they left your office in better shape than they came, their trust in you was solidified.

NOW

Today, trust is built through researching online reviews, checking out the activity on your Facebook page, and visiting your website. Even when someone learns of your practice through a friend or family member, they are going to look you up online. If your reviews are old, your website is painfully antiquated, and social media pages include very few posts, they're not going to be confident in your ability to provide the care they need.

When you use online resources to keep your patients apprised of new technologies and skill sets, they're more likely to put their teeth in your hands. Once they're in your office, you have yet another opportunity to convince them that you're the real deal and perhaps even convince them to commit to a treatment you know they'd benefit from.

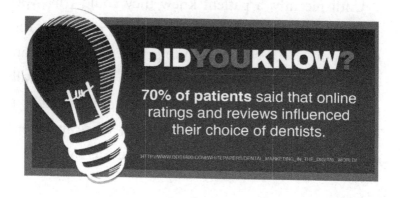

DID YOU KNOW?

70% of patients said that online ratings and reviews influenced their choice of dentists.

HTTP://WWW.DDS1400.COM/WHITEPAPERS/DENTAL_MARKETING_IN_THE_DIGITAL_WORLD/

QUALITY CARE

THEN

A decade ago, quality care meant no marketing. The top dentists felt it was taboo to promote themselves. They believed that if you were a good dentist, there was no need to shout it from the rooftops because your existing patients would spread the word and the new patients would follow. If someone wasn't happy, they'd mutter their discontent to a friend or two and it would be over. Those who did market themselves were believed to provide lower-end services or, even worse, to be pretentious and showy.

NOW

Your patients live online; if they're not in front of a monitor, they've got a tablet or a smartphone in their hands. They use this technology to help them make every decision, from which restaurant to frequent to which oil diffuser is the best.

"Words on the street" are forgotten. Why should they bother trying to remember which friend said what about whom when they can do a simple online search to learn about the kind of care you provide your patients?

Your homepage, Google reviews, video testimonials and Facebook posts tell them everything they need to know in order to pick your practice or move on to the next search result.

Keep in mind that today research is instant. Because information is at their fingertips, consumers can pop online at any time to find the quality of care they're looking for. They will read ads, evaluate blogs, pour over websites, and scour reviews.

In order to show these prospective patients that you provide quality care, it's necessary to include certification logos on your website, write blog posts about continuing education courses you have attended, and feature new equipment on your Facebook page that explains how it can benefit patients.

DIDYOU**KNOW**?

One-third of patients say their choice of dentists is greatly influenced by the quality of the practice's website.

HTTP://WWW.DDS1800.COM/WHITEPAPERS/DENTAL_MARKETING_IN_THE_DIGITAL_WORLD/

HIGHLY SKILLED
"PROFESSIONAL" DOCTORS

THEN

In 2007, you could emphasize your professionalism and skill set by being formal, stuffy, and by showing none of your actual personality. After a perfunctory handshake and a head nod, you would get down to business, never letting on that you were a human with interests and feelings. This was the modus operandi of most professionals, as it was believed that a cold formality was what was expected of them. The idea of showing their authentic personality was unheard of.

NOW

If trust was built on professionalism in 2007, it's now built on authenticity. If you act like an animatronic human from a Disney World attraction, your patients aren't going to have much confidence in your skill set. When you show genuine human emotions, speak to your patients authentically, and share a bit of your personality (and that of your practice) with your patients, they're more open to you and the treatments you recommend.

Times have changed. The people behind Google, Amazon, Netflix, and Facebook aren't wearing suits and ties, they're wearing jeans and sandals; their respect doesn't come from what they wear, but the fact that they're willing to show their employees, shareholders, and consumers that they are human. They have families, enjoy a good laugh, and find countless other ways to relate to "real people."

In addition to emphasizing their skills and qualifications via a professional website and other channels, dentists today need to adapt their demeanor and interactions with patients to appeal to modern expectations.

WORD OF MOUTH

THEN

Word of mouth was simple: A patient would have either a positive or negative opinion about you, your practice or the treatment they received and they would pass it along to friends and family at reunions, barbecues, and little league games.

Those who interpreted the information as positive asked for a number; those who didn't quickly forgot your name. No fuss, no muss. Even if someone learned about your practice through a newspaper advertisement or billboard, the only way they could find out if you were good was through word of mouth. The Internet wasn't the indispensable asset it is today.

NOW

Word of mouth now is conveyed digitally. Sure, your patients may tell others about you. But, ultimately these potential patients are going to do their due diligence online before reaching out to schedule an appointment.

They'll look at reviews left on your practice's Facebook page and on Google to determine whether or not they're willing to take a chance on you. When someone goes online to research your practice, they'll see an assortment of glowing reviews that make them confident in your abilities. Digital word of mouth is also conveyed when someone comments on a Facebook post, forwards one of your emails or blogs to someone, or screenshots an online ad.

PRACTICE PERSONALITY

THEN

Dentists preferred to convey a formal, even stuffy personality. The belief was that their sterile, rigid demeanor would portray professionalism. Even their office decor would reflect frigidity. There would be very few decorations, magazine subscriptions would be conservative, and other details would remind patients that they were in a doctor's office, nothing more. A decade ago, patients associated this austerity with someone who was highly-skilled.

NOW

Your patients want to know that you're like them. If you're a robot in a while coat, they're going to move along to the next dentist that actually appears to be human.

Patients want to know that you're flawed, that you struggle with the same issues they struggle with, and that you have your own personality that is reflected in your practice, including both your office and your team members.

Are you a sports fan? Show it! Do you love rock music? Decorate your office with music memorabilia! Sharing your interests is a great way to connect with your patients. Patients want to be able to relate. If they're into technology, then a practice that offers state-of-the-art treatment will feel like the best fit; if they love to feel pampered, then a dimly lit office with a spa-like atmosphere will speak to them.

When it comes right down to it, the personality you convey online—through your website, emails, blog posts, and Facebook —is what sets you apart from the dentist down the street.

DIDYOUKNOW?

86% of consumers prefer an authentic and honest brand personality on social networks. (Sprout Social, 2016)

SOURCE: HTTPS://WWW.HUBSPOT.COM/MARKETING-STATISTICS

ACCESSIBILITY TO DENTISTRY

THEN

In 2007, few people outside of the profession had access to information about dentistry. At best, an online search would yield a handful of results from questionable sources. Information about dental "tools" were limited to brushing and flossing implements, mouthwashes, and whitening strips. If someone had a legitimate question or dental concern, there was really only one place to turn—an actual dentist.

NOW

If you do a quick Google search on "bleeding gums," you'll meet with 18,900,000 results, give or take. When people have a question or a problem, the first place they turn is the Internet. And while the sources might still be sketchy, many of them are from names that your patients trust, like WebMD and the American Dental Association.

Thanks to services like Smile Direct and Amazon Prime, people now have almost immediate access to cheap aligner trays, light–activated whitening systems like AuraGlow, and even dental extraction kits!

Because patients can access these things without ever leaving the comfort of their beds, it's more important than ever for you to be in front of your patients digitally—if for no other reason than to educate them about why they should not purchase an extraction kit to keep around the house!

DID YOU **KNOW?**

Social media and video viewing are the two most popular online activities. (Smart Insights, 2018)

SOURCE: HTTPS://WWW.HUBSPOT.COM/MARKETING-STATISTICS

ATTRACTING NEW TEAM MEMBERS

THEN

In the first decade of the century, if you wanted to add a team member to your practice, you would maybe place an ad in the local paper, consult a job placement agency, or maybe ask your existing team if they knew anyone who was interested. When you brought someone in for an interview, the only way for them to get a sense of what it would be like to work for you was to take in your office decor, observe how you interacted with others, and maybe evaluate your success based on the number of bodies in your reception area. Whether or not they accepted a position was based mostly on gut instinct.

NOW

Hiring is much easier, thanks to the web. You can place ads on Facebook, employment sites, and even mention on your website that you're hiring.

When potential new hires learn about your practice, they will immediately go online to check out your reputation. They'll look at your website to see if it's up–

to–date and what treatments you offer, they'll go to your Google reviews to see what patients have been saying, and they'll even go to your practice's Facebook page to see how many "likes" and "shares" you have.

What they find online ultimately determines whether they'll contact you for an interview or not.

PATIENT LOYALTY

THEN

In the early 2000s, the market wasn't quite as saturated as it is now. For the most part, people would go to the dentist who was most convenient to their home or office. They knew there were other dentists, but because information about these other practices wasn't readily available their selection was mostly based on convenience. Patient loyalty wasn't such a concern until new practices started cropping up all over the place.

NOW

Private or corporate, there is a dental practice on nearly every street corner. With so many options, people can afford to be more selective when they commit to a dentist. If you don't give them a reason to stay, they can go to someone within a one–mile radius who will.

This makes it more important than ever to make personal connections with your patients regularly through digital means such as Facebook and email. If you aren't staying in front of them, making yourself relatable, and reminding them that you're available for whatever they may need, you'll lose them to another dentist.

DISTRACTIONS

THEN

Up until 2007, we were still using flip phones. Those who were savvy enough to text were using the digital keypads to get their messages through. If you wanted to look up something on "the web" or send an email, you'd have to find a computer. If you didn't have one at home, you'd go to a public library or internet cafe.

Google was already the #1 search engine in the country, but it wasn't yet being used for ads or remarketing. If you wanted to reach an audience and weren't worried about being judged by the dental community for blatantly advertising, you'd purchase a TV or radio spot and hope to reach the right people at the right time.

People were used to waiting in 2007—for return phone calls, information, even an internet connection, in some cases.

Then a major shift occurred when Steve Jobs introduced the iPhone. While there were other smartphone prototypes, the iPhone was the first cellular device to do, well—everything! That singular device can be credited for changing consumer behavior.

NOW

For over a decade, we've had access to several generations of iPhones, Blackberries, and Samsung Galaxies. No computer? No problem, because you've got one in your hand. Smartphones have given us instant access to everything: photography, video, Internet, games, rideshares, food. Instant gratification has become the norm. Why wait around for a taxi when you can just order up an Über?

How does this affect you?

It puts pressure on you to have the information your consumers are looking for readily available, but it also allows you to target more narrowly. Television ads and billboards cast a wide net, but Google ads and web design can be calibrated to reach a very specific audience.

COMPETITION

THEN

While there were plenty of dentists in 2007, there weren't enough to create a genuine competition. Because of how little marketing was done in the industry, patients generally chose to go to the dentist that was in close proximity to home or work. If another practice opened up shop nearby, they weren't perceived as a threat.

NOW

If you stand at a major intersection, you could conceivably have a dentist at each corner, all vying for the same business. Private or corporate, they are all competing for patients. And as unique as your practice is, it's up to you to make sure that consumers know what sets you apart from the others.

Remember that practices backed by corporations are able to spend more on marketing, which puts pressure on you to make sure your marketing efforts are resonating with the right people. The flip side of this is that it also gives you the opportunity to shine a spotlight on your practice, make a connection with your patients, and share a little bit of your personality with them.

Before you start to feel overwhelmed by the idea of this much change, think about this. When you are given the opportunity to incorporate a new piece of equipment (technology) into your practice, you may be hesitant, but you're willing to give it a try for the good of your patients; why would you be skeptical of trying digital marketing? You've got it in ya'—just follow that instinct.

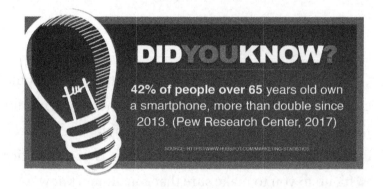

DIDYOU**KNOW**?

42% of people over 65 years old own a smartphone, more than double since 2013. (Pew Research Center, 2017)

SOURCE: HTTP://WWW.HUBSPOT.COM/MARKETING-STATISTICS

DR. JONES MAKES SOME CHANGES

You will remember we introduced Dr. Jones at the beginning of the book. He had come to realize that none of his "traditional" marketing methods were producing the results he needed to improve the quality of his practice.

Dr. Jones decided it was time to overcome his fears and take an important step forward in his career. He knew that marketing his dental practice correctly and effectively was crucial to attracting patients who were looking for his unique skills and treatment offerings. He also came to realize that he should turn this project over to a professional marketing agency (My Dental Agency) to ensure the best outcome in the most cost–effective way.

My Dental Agency prepared a marketing strategy for Dr. Jones that incorporated all the digital marketing platforms and tools currently available to present a seamless, comprehensive image of him and his practice.

We customized his plan to present the unique personality of his practice while showcasing his skills and credentials to attract the type of patients that he wanted to serve.

Some of the things that were included in his plan:

- A website that resonates with the patients he wants to treat because it represents the practice personality and is not a cookie–cutter site made from a template.

- Adding a blog to the website to build authority and trust.

- Adding patient video testimonials to his website that backed up his qualifications with their candid assessment of his skills and their satisfaction with their completed treatment.

- Incentives to drive patients to add reviews to his website and important review sites like Google and Facebook. These reviews give new patient prospects a feel for the practice and show them that they could expect outstanding care and treatment from Dr. Jones and his team.

- Ads on Facebook and Google to create awareness of the practice that were also targeted to attract the patients Dr. Jones wanted to treat.

- Facebook and Google ads also pointed potential patients to a well-designed landing page where they could learn more about the practice and even make appointments.

- Email marketing to patients to deepen the relationships, educate their current patients to drive more value, and leverage their patients to get in front of their friends and family.

- Creating and synchronizing local business listings to increase online visibility.

Dr. Jones feels that the customized digital marketing campaign provided by My Dental Agency delivered much higher value results for his financial investment when compared to traditional marketing methods, and he is very pleased with the results of his "digital makeover."

LET'S GET DIGITAL!

DENTALDISRUPTION.COM/CALL

If you've been resisting the transition from traditional marketing to digital, hesitate no more. My Dental Agency has helped countless dentists just like you make the leap. What's more, we're in it for the long haul. From your initial FREE breakthrough session to achieving the vision you've always had for your practice, we'll be there with you. You'll have more time to do what you're great at, and we'll take care of the rest.

Contact us today at DentalDisruption.com/call

CHAPTER FOUR

The Marketing Disruptions That Are a Detriment to Your Practice

CHAPTER FOUR

The Marketing Disruptions That Are
a Detriment to Your Practice

In the hypothetical scenario I used in my introduction, you learned that what Dr. Jones was using to market his practice was not as effective as it used to be. But instead of continuing with his old methods with a dogged determination to stay the same, he was willing to adapt to new methods that would ultimately ensure the success of his practice.

Now most practices realize that marketing is necessary. But it's one thing to know how marketing has changed over the past ten years, and it's an entirely different ballgame when it comes to making adjustments that will transform your practice.

In this chapter we will highlight the major marketing disruptions that are hampering your success and suggest methods that will help your practice thrive.

HAVING A WEBSITE—BUT NO TRAFFIC

Imagine building a resort in a lush but secluded woods. You wait for guests to show up, but you forgot one important thing—directions. In this analogy, your website is the resort and your other marketing efforts—emails, Facebook posts, Google and Facebook ads and reviews—all point your patients in the right direction. While websites for dental practices were few and far between in 2007, they are now the norm, and they need to be seen.

At this point, most dental practices have a website, but that is not enough. It's a good start if you've invested in a website that your competitors will envy. Vibrant colors, photos that show you and your team members interacting with patients, video testimonials, and easy-to–navigate subpages are FANTASTIC—unless no one sees them.

All of your marketing efforts should result in a visit to your website. If no one sees your site, then why bother keeping it up-to-date? Having a website does not guarantee that it will be seen by your target audience—just like owning a resort will not guarantee that it will be occupied by guests.

The only way to make your website an effective marketing tool is to ensure that it actually gets seen. Emails, Facebook, reviews, and online advertisements need to function like bright neon "THIS WAY" signs.

NOT UTILIZING SOCIAL MEDIA TO CONNECT WITH PATIENTS

In 2007, social media wasn't even an option for marketing. Sure, MySpace was thriving and FaceBook was in its infancy, but both were strictly for personal use.

These days, everyone from your nephew to your great-aunt uses social media to stay in touch with those they care about. If you don't put yourself in front of your patients on sites such as Facebook, you're missing out on an opportunity to connect with them!

In fact, social media is one of the easiest ways to share your real personality with your patients. Whether you include video of yourself drawing the name of a raffle winner or a picture of your team members delivering teacher appreciation treats to the local middle school, Facebook is the ideal platform for getting in front of current and potential patients. Facebook provides readers the option to digest information one brief post at a time. You can build rapport by simply sharing photos, memes, videos, or links to your latests blogs or website content.

USING TEMPLATED CONTENT

Picture this: You're looking for a doctor to help with neck and back problems that have developed after hunching over patients day in and day out for so many years. You do a cursory Google search and start clicking on the results.

The first site looks great. It's got a picture of a spinal x–ray, smiling patients, and details about the practice, so it goes on your "maybe" list. The second site looks, well... the same. The color scheme and fonts are different, but the pictures and the copy are the same as the first. How is doctor two different from doctor one? Now, both doctors are crossed off your list.

Why would you commit to a practice that tells you NOTHING about their team members, their genuine mission statement, and what they're all about? Ultimately, you're going to pick the doctor who has fresh content, pictures of real patients, and uses customized copy that speaks to who they are and how their treatment benefits you.

In 2007, templated material was the norm. Most people didn't realize that they were seeing canned content and if they did, they didn't care. Ultimately, using templated material may still be easy, but it is NOT ideal. This is particularly important when it comes to attracting new patients.

If all roads lead to your website, then your site should contain personalized content that sets you apart from other dentists in your area—especially corporate practices. Much to the chagrin of corporate marketing agencies, templated content is, well…transparent! Even with a referral, a potential patient is going to judge you by your digital footprint; if the text on your site is exactly the same as ten other sites that they see, you won't be taken seriously.

DID YOU KNOW?

59% of Americans believe that customer service through social media has made it easier to get their questions answered and issues resolved. (Lyfe Marketing, 2018)

SOURCE: HTTPS://WWW.HUBSPOT.COM/MARKETING-STATISTICS

FAILURE TO USE DIGITAL MARKETING

Digital marketing is the only way to stay in front of your patients and appeal to anyone looking for a dentist just like you.

Unlike ads on billboards, radio, MailPak, or bus benches, digital marketing is easier to track. When you know which marketing campaigns are or are not working, you can modify your campaigns so that they reach the patients you've been looking for.

Best of all, digital marketing can be more cost effective. When information is almost immediately available it's easy to make changes that give you the biggest return on your investment. And you won't have to pay for printing and postage to send four different postcards to 6000 new home buyers in your area!16-DYK#9

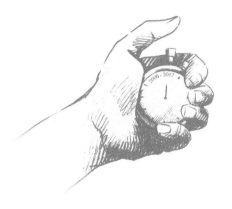

CHAPTER FIVE

Client Success Stories

CHAPTER FIVE

Client Success Stories

I interviewed a couple of my clients to learn how the digital transition affected them and their practices. Their stories are compelling. It's extremely meaningful to read about how the changes that have occurred over the last decade have affected other dentists.

DR. RUTH MORGAN, DDS
Canton, Mississippi

Dr. Morgan graduated from the LSU School of Dentistry in 1982. For two years, she taught at the Medical College of Georgia and then went to work for a private practice owner in Canton, Mississippi. At that time, female dentists did not enjoy the same respect as their male counterparts, so her initial experience was a challenge. The dentist she worked for had inconsistent expectations and that helped to make private practice an attractive option.

Dr. Morgan decided to strike out on her own in 1985. She moved to a new building where she could thrive. At that time mentoring was relatively rare. The only advice she received about marketing was from a continuing education course. Their advice? To hang a shingle, preferably one that could be seen at night. At that point, few dentists even had signage, so something that simple could give her an edge on her limited competition.

Fast-forward to 2005. At the time, the Yellow Pages were the best way to find a new business. In its heyday, the Yellow Pages was comprised of a three-inch tome—in bigger cities two separate books—of local listings. The best marketing advice Dr. Morgan received was to get the biggest ad she could afford.

Her practice had a website—probably the only one in the area at the time—but it was basic. She recalls a local chiropractor who purchased a billboard. He was perceived as unprofessional, cheesy, and—worst of all— desperate to "sink" to that level. That was not necessarily her opinion, but a reflection of the climate at the time.

By the time Dr. Morgan shifted from Yellow Pages to digital, she was pretty much on board. She knew that paper was dead. Additionally, the patients who came in as a result of Yellow Pages or radio ads weren't the quality patients she was interested in. While she did promote her practice through local newspapers and newsletters, those efforts were more about face and brand recognition.

Now that she's been digital for several years, she recognizes it as the "biggest bang for the buck." "Digital is less expensive, reaches more people, and can be more selective than other marketing efforts," she said.

Digital allows dentists to provide more material and information than print ever allowed. Dr. Morgan realizes that digital is simply more efficient; even with a referral, potential patients are going to go online to research her practice. Ten years ago, consumers were limited, but now they're educated. They are savvy and want to know why YOUR practice is better than the one that is closer and cheaper.

Dr. Morgan experienced a major change in the formality of the profession. When she first entered dentistry, dentists dressed and acted in a way that could be interpreted as stodgy and unfriendly. In fact, while at the LSU School of Dentistry, she was told that she would never make it in private practice because she was too personable, too open, too conversive, and not nearly professional enough. Now, these traits actually serve to help her make genuine connections with her patients. Her reviews and testimonials frequently reference her warm personality and how comfortable she makes patients feel, proving that allowing others to see her human side has played a major role in the success of her practice.

With an influx of corporate dentistry and insurance-driven dental care, it is more important than ever that high-quality dental practices like yours and Dental Solutions of Mississippi prove themselves to their consumers.

"Corporate practices have massive amounts of money to put towards advertising, but if you don't educate the consumer about the differences between them and your high-quality private practice, the only difference they're going to notice is that you're more expensive," Dr. Morgan said.

Sure, you could market to consumers who are looking for discount dentistry, but are they going to be returning patients who are invested in the long-term health of their teeth? No! They're going to move on to the next dentist who promotes their practice via Groupon, LivingSocial, and Woot.

Dr. Morgan realized sooner than others that digital is the only way to keep up. What you posted last week is old news; only digital allows you to stay in front of your patients in a way that keeps your practice relevant.

My Dental Agency Google Campaign

for Dr. Morgan

Objective

The Google campaign was targeted toward higher caliber services such as Implants and Cosmetic Dentistry. We did not want to attract only new patients looking for an exam. Our ads were focused on patients who were looking for larger treatments to be completed and a qualified dentist to do them. Because the ads were focused more narrowly, the volume of responses wouldn't be as high as an ad for a $79 cleaning and exam. Ads with laser–like focus are important to the client because they want to attract quality patients. They are willing to get a lower volume of patients for a higher–quality, more qualified patient.

Result

13 Month Campaign Result

109 Implant Leads
8.38 leads per month

- 109 conversions (new patient leads) over 13 months

- 8.38 leads per month average

*My Dental Agency prepared and managed additional campaigns and services for Dr. Morgan. This is only one example.

My Dental Agency Website Development

for Dr. Morgan*

Dr. Morgan's practice not only used technology that no other dentists in their area were using, they were also using both online and offline marketing strategies. The problem was they also had an extremely outdated website that did not tell their unique story or inform visitors about their unique services.

We completely renovated their website. The new website showcased the practice personality, told how they were unique and focused on how their unique technology benefited patients.

Before

*My Dental Agency prepared and managed additional campaigns and services for Dr. Morgan. This is only one example.

My Dental Agency Reputation Management

for Dr. Morgan*

In spite of being much beloved by patients, this top–notch team had received a couple of negative reviews. They had been using companies like RateABiz, but with little to no strategy.

We worked with them to manage their reputation. In a few short months they went from 9 reviews averaging 4.1 to over 20 reviews averaging 4.5!

★★★★☆
9 Reviews / 4.1 Star Rating

★★★★☆
20 Reviews / 4.5 Star Rating

— As of today! —
★★★★★
53 Reviews / 4.7 Star Rating

Update: As our campaign continues, Dr. Morgan has gathered more excellent reviews. Since our last report she has reached a total of 53 reviews averaging 4.7!

*My Dental Agency prepared and managed additional campaigns and services for Dr. Morgan. This is only one example.

My Dental Agency Rebranding for Dr. Morgan*

Dr. Morgan was rebranding her practice and wanted her current patients to be comfortable with the change. This was also an opportunity to let the local community learn more about what this amazing practice had to offer. We decided the best way to do this was through a 53-second video ad.

In a single month the ad received 5,100 3-second views, 2,873 10-second views, and 341 100% views. It also earned 97 clicks, which means that 97 people were interested in learning more about the practice.

Video Results for 1 Month

5,100 - 3-Second Views
2,873 - 10-Second Views
341 - 100% Views
97 - Clicks

*My Dental Agency prepared and managed additional campaigns and services for Dr. Morgan. This is only one example.

DR. MICHELLE MUNOZ, DDS
Uvalde, Texas

Dr. Munoz graduated from dental school in May of 2001. By the following month she had been hired as an associate at a dental practice in Dallas. She longed to be closer to family and when she learned that her father's dentist was interested in retiring, she moved home to Uvalde, Texas. There, she worked as Dr. Carr's associate for about a year. When he retired in 2002, Dr. Munoz purchased his practice and she has been at that location ever since.

Marketing a dental practice was never discussed. It was not covered in dental school, nor did the doctor she worked for in Dallas offer any advice. When she purchased Dr. Carr's practice, his advertising consisted of an ad in the Yellow Pages and a toll–free number for patients to call. His only advice to her was to keep both.

At that time, the perception was that it looked desperate for dentists to advertise their practices. It seemed the only ones who really advertised were dentists who wanted to work in bulk, essentially, churning patient after patient through with little personalization or customized care.

As the digital landscape began to change, Dr. Munoz began to soften her attitude about advertising. She was perplexed about the entire concept, though, because she did not have social network accounts and spent very little time online in general.

It took her awhile to understand the impact that Facebook, Google, and online reviews were having on businesses, but she realized that digital marketing was becoming more common and necessary. Her younger team members eventually convinced her to give it a chance. Not only was she thrilled by the results digital marketing had on her practice, she was also surprised by becoming more tech–savvy than she had ever been.

Part of the reason this shift was necessary was because patients were becoming better informed through the Internet. Patients had questions for their medical practitioners and were no longer afraid to ask. They would spend hours researching practices, reputations, and treatments and expected to be treated with kindness, patience, and respect instead of being spoken down to. Today, if patients don't feel a connection with their dentist, they'll move on to someone else.

Change can be difficult, and it was no different for Dr. Munoz. As a mentor to new dentists, she advises that they start with digital marketing in order to get the most "bang for their buck." She has been thrilled with the results of her marketing campaigns and has even been successful enough to open a second practice dedicated specifically to sleep dentistry and TMD treatment. As with her dental practice, her new center will reach patients through digital marketing.

My Dental Agency Facebook Campaign

for Dr. Munoz*

Objective

Promote sleep apnea treatments and Dr. Munoz'
practice through Facebook one Facebook ad

Results

- 150 leads for sleep/TMD in 5 months

- 105 page likes in 5 months

- 296,654 impressions in 5 months

- 35,658 reach in 5 months

This is a very impressive response for one Facebook
ad.

5 Month Campaign Results

150 - Sleep/TMD Leads
105 - Page Likes
296,654 - Impressions
35,658 - Reached

*My Dental Agency prepared and manages many additional campaigns and services for Dr. Munoz. This is only one example.

CHAPTER SIX

Marketing Campaign Success Stories

CHAPTER SIX

Marketing Campaign Success Stories

My Dental Agency has a proven track record of creating and executing successful marketing campaigns for our clients. We have shared a few of those successes with you on the following pages. Please be aware that we have changed the names of each practice to protect their privacy.

RIVERSIDE DENTAL*
Pay-Per-Click Campaign

Riverside was a well–established practice when they came to us for help. Although they had been in the community for a long time, they wanted now to focus on growing their Implant and Invisalign cases. One of the strategies we agreed upon was to run paid ads for both of these services on Google.

These ads led to 114 total leads, 10 of which resulted in patient treatments (proven to come directly from this campaign) that earned the practice an additional $22,500 of revenue.

Campaign Results

114 - Leads

10 - Implant / Invisalign Cases

$22,500 - Revenue

*Name changed to protect privacy

THE SCHAEFER CENTER*

Schaefer Center engaged us to do a comprehensive "makeover" of their digital footprint. We prepared a plan that encompassed every facet of their marketing strategy. We present four of the areas we addressed on the following pages.

*Name changed to protect privacy

THE SCHAEFER CENTER*
Reputation Management

The Schaefer Center had experienced a couple of negative reviews. While every practice we talk to has indicated that they, too, get negative reviews, these reviews were keeping the team up at night. We made reputation management a priority and worked diligently at building a more positive online presence.

The results? Within a single year this practice went from 10 Facebook reviews averaging 3.3 stars to 33 reviews averaging 4.5 stars.

facebook.

★★★☆☆
10 Reviews / 3.3 Star Rating
October 2016

★★★★☆
33 Reviews / 4.5 Star Rating
October 2017

*Name changed to protect privacy

THE SCHAEFER CENTER*
Quality vs. Quantity

This practice wanted to attract more quality patients–patients willing to invest in their dental health and wanting to establish a long–term relationship with the doctor. We knew they needed to be more strategic with their marketing. We created Google ads that targeted very specific services and emphasized words like "premier" and "quality."

This campaign generated a $15,000 case within the first three leads!

Campaign Results

$15,000 Revenue
in the first 3 leads

*Name changed to protect privacy

THE SCHAEFER CENTER*
Local Awareness Ad on Facebook

Dr. Schaefer didn't have much of a digital presence and wasn't doing much advertising, either. We knew we initially needed to focus on increasing brand awareness and showcasing how his practice was unique.

Within three months, the Facebook ad led to 81,575 impressions with 22,773 people reached. Best of all, 94 people clicked indicating that they wanted to learn more.

3 Month Campaign Results

81,575 - Impressions
22,773 - People Reached
94 - Clicks

*Name changed to protect privacy

THE SCHAEFER CENTER*
Showcasing a Unique Practice

This practice truly changes patients' lives and they received many thank-you cards from their patients on a regular basis. The problem was that all this positive feedback wasn't reflected on their original website.

Dr. Schaefer's website needed to be more clear and concise, but we also needed to showcase exactly how Dr. Schaefer changed the lives of his patients. We revamped the site to include testimonials and photos of patient transformations, providing proof of his ability and how his patients felt about him.

*Name changed to protect privacy

YOUR FAMILY DENTAL*
Capitalizing on Technology

This long-time dentist had purchased an existing practice prior to working with us but felt like he was starting all over. We learned he was using Smile Prevue in his practice. We built an ad campaign around this advantage, which provided the perfect opportunity to drive cosmetic dentistry patients to the practice.

Our SmileMakeover and Invisalign Google campaigns generated a $10,250 case within the first four months of running the ads.

Campaign Results
$10,250 Case
in the first 4 months

*Name changed to protect privacy

BASSETT DENTAL SOLUTIONS*
Facebook Invisalign Campaign

This dentist wanted to bring in more Invisalign patients. Part of our strategy to do that included creating a Facebook campaign with a narrow focus.

In two months, 4,626 people were reached, 67 clicked to learn more, and 2 form submissions were completed.

2 Month Campaign Results

4,626 - People Reached

67 - Clicks

2 - Form Submissions

*Name changed to protect privacy

DR. MARK DAVIS*
Google and Facebook Campaigns

This practice has spent a great amount of money on marketing through the years. They marketed digitally and traditionally (radio, newspaper, postcards) but were not getting the quality leads they wanted. Dr. Davis engaged My Dental Agency to revamp their approach to marketing the practice. As one component of our complete plan, we initiated a comprehensive marketing campaign for them online that included, among other initiatives, Google and Facebook ads.

Objective

Target ads to attract patients interested in obtaining quality treatments such as dental implants.

Results

Google Campaign

- 264 conversions over 12 months

- average 22 conversions per month

Facebook Implant Campaign

- 24 leads

- $13.53 average per lead

Google Campaign (12 Months)

264 - Conversions
22 - Average Per Month

Facebook Implant Campaign

24 - Leads
$13.53 - Average Per Lead

*Name changed to protect privacy

PROVEN RESULTS!

My Dental Agency has successfully utilized the digital market to help dentists all over the nation grow their practices and meet their business goals. These stories illustrate only a few pieces of the overall marketing puzzle. Our strategy is comprehensive, ensuring that websites, ads, Facebook, and reputation management work together for the benefit of our clients. Let us create a custom marketing plan to meet your needs today!

LET'S GET DIGITAL!

DENTALDISRUPTION.COM/CALL

If you've been resisting the transition from traditional marketing to digital, hesitate no more. My Dental Agency has helped countless dentists just like you make the leap. What's more, we're in it for the long haul. From your initial FREE breakthrough session to achieving the vision you've always had for your practice, we'll be there with you. You'll have more time to do what you're great at, and we'll take care of the rest.

Contact us today at DentalDisruption.com/call

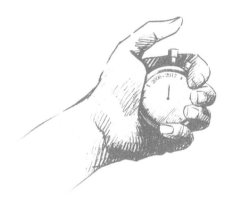

CHAPTER SEVEN

A Final Word

CHAPTER SEVEN

A Final Word

Technology changes faster than most people change their minds. Once you've embraced technology, you should be prepared to continue being adaptive. After all, the future might include livestreamed patient consultations prior to treatment, asking "Alexa" or "Siri" to tell patients which dentist has the earliest available appointment, or even educating patients about their treatment through the use of virtual reality. Be willing to at least consider whatever the future might bring.

While the story of Dr. Jones was intended to be fun and informational, I see stories just like his happening every day. Better to recognize the importance of digital marketing now than regret not doing so in the future.

Although things have changed, they've changed for the better. Patients are typically more educated, and this change gives us the opportunity to use fun and inventive methods when marketing dental practices. Without the formality and stuffiness that we used to encounter, we can now think out of the box and create innovative marketing material that will help dentists achieve their goals and patients to find the care they've been looking for.

There is still value to the methods used prior to 2018, but they are ideal when integrated with contemporary digital marketing. Without an online presence, you simply won't keep up with the competitors that take advantage of technology to make sure they're on the minds of their patients.

Ultimately, your patients are no different from other human beings. They crave connection. Digital technology is a low–risk way for you to give them what they need, retain your current patients, and still attract the new patients that will allow your practice to thrive. If you're still stuck in 2007 and have no desire to grow your practice, then you just may be left in the dust.

Seeing Opportunities and Planning for the Future

The difference between an "okay" practice and an "excellent" practice can be as simple as seeing and taking advantage of opportunities for growth. The difference between dreaming of a thriving practice, full life, and a beautiful retirement in the future and enjoying them requires not only recognizing opportunities, but also acting to turn those dreams into reality.

Make the Most of Opportunities to Serve Patients and Grow Your Practice

The top reasons adults cite for avoiding the dentist include: *

Cost

59% of adults indicated they forgo dental care due to cost.

Fear of the dentist

22% of adults cited fear of the dentist to explain avoiding appointments.

Inability to find convenient location or appointment time

19% reported they could not find a convenient location and/or time for appointments.

You should view these statistics as opportunities for you to reach these underserved patients with information that shows how your practice can help them. A good marketing plan will include strategies to address each of these points (fears) by addressing them head–on with solutions you offer.

Many potential patients do not realize that there is a difference in the quality of care they may receive from different providers. They may not believe that they should invest financially in their own dental wellbeing. These perceptions and concern about the cost of potential dental treatment can lead patients to select a provider who appears to be the least expensive alternative. A good marketing campaign will showcase the quality care you provide and subtly illuminate the reasons that cheaper is not always better when it comes to their dental health care. Providing information about financial arrangements available to them may or may not be included in the marketing campaign, depending upon your business model.

There are many patients who are simply afraid of visits to the dentist. Rather than ignore this fact, your marketing campaign can begin to put them at ease before they reach your office. Highlighting one or two techniques you use to help them relax and providing testimonials from former "fearful patients" can help them realize that you are the right choice for their needs.

Potential patients might not realize that your office is "right around the corner" from their home or work. Some will favor locations closer to work, while others will favor those closer to their homes. While you can't be in both locations for each patient, a good marketing campaign will raise awareness of your practice, the services you provide, and where you are located.

*https://www.ada.org/en/science-research/health-policy-institute/dental-statistics/patients

Retirement—at Any Age—Is Just a Wish Unless You Act to Make It Happen

No one wants to work forever, so retirement is something every dentist should plan for. There are several factors that dictate when a dentist retires. Retirement may result from a desire to retire at a certain age, personal or family health issues, economic pressures, economic success, and more.

Studies show that the average retirement age for dentists is increasing. In the ten–year period from 2007 to 2017, the average retirement age increased from 67.1 to 68.9 years.* Why is this number increasing?

One reason for the increase is that some older dentists facing retirement begin to realize they have not reached their potential. They do not have enough resources reserved to fund the retirement of their dreams. So, they extend the date of their planned retirement in order to make up the shortfall. Then they realize that extending their years of work won't increase their profits unless something else changes. They need more patients and/ or increased patient values. That is when they call us to see if a marketing program might help them to achieve their goals.

As of 2017, there were 61.0 dentists working in dentistry per 100,000 US population.**

This is great because it means that dental care is now available to more of the US population than ever before. However, in many areas there are now too many dental providers available for the number of potential patients. If you are in one of these areas it means that it is even more important that you have a strategic marketing campaign that makes your practice stand out from the crowd.

*Dentist Retirement Patterns (Health Policy Institute Infographic

**Ratios vary by state. Source: Supply of Dentists in the US: 2001-2017 (Tables in Excel)

https://www.ada.org/en/science-research/health-policy-institute/dental-statistics/workforce

Capitalizing on Opportunities, creating a Plan, and Acting to Get Results

Remaining up–to–date is imperative as new medical and technological innovations, clinical practices, and more change the dental landscape. Remaining competitive depends not only upon staying up with current practices, but also providing potential patients the information they need to determine that your practice is the right place for them. We are here to help you plan and execute a campaign that will help you to achieve your marketing goals.

As I have shared in this book, My Dental Agency works with each doctor to create a marketing campaign to achieve his or her goals. We design entire websites to showcase the practice and provide the information potential patients need to determine that this is the right dentist for them. We analyze the market and prepare campaigns to get the message out to potential patients where they are most likely to be contacted—on social media. We help them to present themselves in a professional yet friendly manner that attracts quality patients.

When you entrust your marketing needs to My Dental Agency, we will provide a complete solution tailored to your unique practice and needs. Some of the many services we provide include:

- Website redevelopment

- Website maintenance

- Google & Facebook review solicitation

- Local business directory listing creation & synchronization

- Monthly blogging

- Facebook page management

- Posting, engagement and images

- Facebook ad management

- Monthly email campaign

- Targeted email campaigns

- Google Pay-Per-Click management

- Google & Facebook remarketing

My Dental Agency Is the Best Choice

to

Help You Achieve Your Marketing Goals!

Jackie Ulasewich, CEO
My Dental Agency

With over a decade of experience in corporate dental laboratory marketing, Jackie Ulasewich decided to take her passion for the dental and marketing industries to the next level by founding My Dental Agency. Since then, she and her team have helped practices all over the country grow their practice through customized, effective marketing campaigns. When she isn't helping dental practices reach their potential, she can be found at home snuggling with her infant daughter Chelsea or spending time outdoors with friends and family.

Made in the USA
Middletown, DE
21 July 2019